Wood, Wind and Water

Library of Congress Cataloging-in-Publication Data

Converse, Anne T., and Ford, Carolyn M.

Wood, Wind and Water, A Story of The Opera House Cup Race of Nantucket/

Selected photographs by Anne T. Converse; text by Carolyn M. Ford

ISBN 0-9714030-0-7

1. Yachts and racing-Pictorial works. 2. Sailing-pictorial works
3. Nantucket-history, text and photographs 4. The Opera House Cup Race-
history in text and photographs 5. Converse, Anne T. 6. Ford, Carolyn M.
6. Photographers-United States 7. Writers-United States

Wood, Wind and Water

A STORY OF THE OPERA HOUSE CUP RACE OF NANTUCKET

To Bob, June 8, 2002
Keep the sailing spirit
alive!

Photographs by Anne T. Converse

Written by Carolyn M. Ford

Anne T. Converse (Annie)

Carolyn M. Ford (Carie)

1983

ACKNOWLEDGEMENTS

*W*e are grateful for the help of the following individuals and organizations, without whom it would not have been possible to give this book a personality. We have listed our friends and supporters in alphabetical order for no other reason than it was the easiest way. Thank you one and all for contributing to our book and making it come alive!

Annie Converse and Camie Ford

Nat Benjamin, Jim Feeney, Huntley F. Fitzpatrick, Guppy Ford, Gwen Gaillard, Ross Gannon, Don Glassie, George Hill, Nick Judson, Barbara Kranichfeld, Diane and Allan LaFrance, Gene Mahon, Herb Marshall, Courtland and Georgia McDonald, Peter McDonald, Elizabeth Meyer, Paul C. Morris, Alfie Sanford, Walter Schank, Lawrence Smart, Davis Taylor, Bob and Elizabeth Tiedeman, Donald Tofias, Chick Walsh, Lawrence Warner, Steve White.

Kristiina Almy for her superb talent in the beautiful design of the book.

James Tierney and Regent Publishing Services for their support and help in printing the book.

The Herreshoff Museum in Bristol, Rhode Island, Mystic Seaport Museum, Mystic, Connecticut, The Nantucket Community Sailing Program, The Opera House Cup Race Committee.

We also thank our ancestors for inspiring us with a love of the sea and the vessels that sail on it:

Harry E. Converse, Captain Mary P. Converse, Roger W. Converse, Roger W. Converse Jr., Costello C. Converse, Edward R. Mitton, Edward J. Mitton.

Shamrock, 1996.

INTRODUCTION

*I*n Hawaii, when a tree is needed for the hull of an outrigger canoe, it can sometimes take weeks for the builder to determine which tree is willing to give itself for the purpose. Some would dismiss this as animism, a primitive form of nature worship in which all parts of the natural world, plants and animals are imbued with individual spirits. For those of us who have a profound attachment to wooden objects, the notion of the living spirit in wood may not be a difficult one with which to identify.

There is sensuality inherent in wooden sailing crafts. Sound, touch, smell, sight, and taste are all stimulated in ways best known to those who share an addiction to the combination of wood, wind, and water. The sound of a wooden hull cutting through the water, the cracking of the timbers, mast and spars, are unique in each vessel. The smell of varnished mahogany or oiled teak dusted with salt spray, the feeling of a wheel rubbed smooth from years of experienced hands steering, the vision of voluminous sails cutting through fog, the sound of luffing jibs; these are all subjective memories which keep a small group of people hooked on spending arduous amounts of time, labor, love and money on their wooden boats. They perceive themselves as custodians of an ancient tradition in which the living tree creates a basic and primal connection for us humans.

This story is for and about people who love wooden boats. Most of them love to sail, some love the sport of yacht racing and others are merely observers, but all share a passion for the construction and preservation of wooden vessels. The older vessels are cared for as one devotedly would care for an elderly member of one's family. When a yacht does change hands the history of the bark is passed on from one owner to the next with awe and reverence. The yachts are restored and maintained as time capsules afloat, expressions of a continuing maritime tradition.

This passion transcends social, economic and cultural lines. The owners are of all ages and walks of life: boatbuilders, yacht brokers, carpenters, lobstermen, businessmen, those with vast incomes and others with just a few pennies to support their habit: old money, new money, young and old, men and women, and families who sail together and pass on the tradition. There are the legendary ones, who have sailed The Opera House Cup Race from the beginning and newcomers who carry on the tradition. The race created the first arena for this loose knit clan of wooden boat owners to compete against one another in a handicap yacht race. The race is fun but also serious enough, as the owners are for the most part avid and skilled racers. Most significantly, The Opera House Cup Race provides an incentive for wooden sailboat owners to congregate every August against the backdrop of Nantucket to show off the efforts of their labor and love.

The Opera House Cup Race highlights both the old and the new. It is about the people and the aesthetic they work to preserve, the fun they have in the process, and the competitive spirit of the race. Profiles of individual yachts and their owners are included so that the reader can better understand the personal nature of the endeavor. There is an overview of the race itself, but in my estimation the greatest thrill is experiencing these boats under sail racing against each other, taking advantage of every puff of wind, every shift of tide and current, and the dramatic variations of the weather. The racing photographs prove the great strength of this book as they bind together the owner and crew to their vessel. Annie Converse's photography speaks for itself in every aspect of this special event, from the dropping of anchors to the celebratory bashes.

This pictorial essay describes classic beauty on the high seas in the setting of The Opera House Cup Race, the precursor of the Classic Yacht Racing Series, which now includes The Emperor's Cup (Marblehead, Massachusetts), the Eggemoggin Reach Regatta (Brooklyn, Maine), The Classic Yacht Regatta (Newport, Rhode Island), The Governor's Cup (Essex, Connecticut), The Mayor's Cup (New York, New York), and The Race Rock Regatta (Stonington, Connecticut). Of this series The Opera House Cup Race stands alone as the mother of all the races. The location, the funky high-brow/low-brow character of Nantucket itself, a rich and often funny history of the race, the retelling of quirky salty yarns from races gone by—all come together to create a flavor-filled event well worth chronicling.

Pride of Baltimore arrives in Nantucket, 1992.

A BRIEF HISTORY OF NANTUCKET

There could be no more perfect venue for a classic yacht regatta than Nantucket, an island, steeped in maritime tradition. The island culture has always revolved around its relationship with the mainland and the sea. Before white men colonized Nantucket in the 17th century, the Indians traveled between the island, the mainland and the sea by dugout canoe. This was a daring means of transportation given the precarious nature of the wind, currents, and shoals.

By the late 18th century a vigorous whaling and coastal shipping trade had developed. By 1774 there were over 4,000 residents living on the island and 150 whaling ships making Nantucket their homeport. A lighthouse at Brandt's Point was first built in 1746. By the end of the century Straight Wharf, Old South Wharf, and Old North Wharf existed as did a lighthouse at Great Point.

Two whaling ships from Nantucket, the *Beaver* and the *Dartmouth*, figured in the Boston Tea Party in 1773 as they returned from delivering whale oil to London, bringing back shipments of tea for the Boston market. During the whaling era ships from Nantucket traveled the globe making the island a recognized name in every foreign port. "By 1823 Nantucket was the leading whaling port in the United States."[1] By 1834 there were five major wharves–New Wharf, Old Wharf, South Wharf, Swain's Wharf, and Commercial Wharf, which was rebuilt of stone in 1850.

By 1840 the population had more than doubled to almost 10,000 people. Between 1840 and 1870 the whaling industry was central to the island's economy, but when the *Eunice H. Adams* retired from service in 1878, the whaling industry came to an end and the population plummeted to 4,123.

With the decline of whaling in the late 19th century, the fishing and scalloping industry became an increasingly important part of the economy. Steamboat travel took over as the primary transportation mode between the mainland and Nantucket in the 1880s. This enabled larger numbers of visitors to come to the island.

"Between July 1, 1883 and July 1, 1884, a total of 21,113 vessels were reported to have passed through Nantucket Sound. Of this number 18,221 were schooners, of the rest 2,247 were steam vessels...The average number of schooners traveling through the sound was about 1,500 per month."[2] As a result of the increase in maritime traffic, shipwrecks increased as well. The shores of Nantucket seemed magnets for passing coastal vessels. The number of ships destroyed in Nantucket waters over the past 100 years is in the hundreds, proving that these can be lethal waters for vessels large and small. In 1874 the first U.S. Life Saving Station was established on Nantucket for the purpose of saving the lives of crew members on board foundering vessels. By 1889 there were three such facilities on the island–Great Neck, Madaket, and Surfside.

By the 1890s the larger sailing ships were a rarity in Nantucket Harbor. During the late 1880s a series of catboats were built to transport passengers up and down the Nantucket coastline, bringing smaller boats into fashion and the concept of charter and leisure sailing into being. People were beginning to come to the island for summer vacations. The seeds of a tourist economy were being planted.

By 1905 the year-round population of the island had dropped to 2,930. Fishing still remained the predominant industry, but the closing of the Nantucket Custom House in 1913 made it impossible for any of the locals to register their boats in Nantucket.

In 1916 a German U-boat sank six steamships off the coast of Nantucket and in 1918 another U-boat sank five fishing vessels and a British steamship off George's Bank. The survivors were brought to Nantucket. As a result of these tragedies, the people of Nantucket became passionately involved in World War I. The Nantucket Yacht Club was taken over as a headquarters for a very active Naval Reserve.

After the war's end, the population had dwindled to 2,797 by 1928. Rum-running became a lucrative source of income for some Nantucketers during Prohibition. Swordfishing from 34-foot sloops became a new source of income. Even though life for the islanders seemed difficult through the 1930s, there was an increased interest in tourism. The Schooner, *Allen Gurney*, was made into a tearoom and restaurant as she greeted visitors. Tied up next to Steamboat Wharf she was a romantic reminder of the shipping history of the island. World War II brought about the same intimate involvement as the previous war. Many privately owned vessels were used for anti-submarine patrol. During the 1940s the fleet of catboats began to disappear and motor-boat charter businesses came into existence.

It was not until the 1970s when Walter Beinecke developed the waterfront, that Nantucket became the showcase of opulent wealth that it is known to be today. Nantucket, wealthy whaling center of the 19th century, impoverished economic community of the late 19th century and first half of the 20th century, was revitalized by the insurgence of tourism. Not only does Nantucket now boast first-class restaurants, hotels and shops but also extraordinary summer houses. The year-round population is back to a healthy 9,000 and real estate on the island is selling at a premium. What makes Nantucket so desirable and unique is its remarkable history, which gives richness and authenticity to a place as solid, rugged, and individualistic as the cobblestones paving its main streets.

This strong Yankee heritage lends substance to the spectacle of classic yacht racing, which takes place there each August. It is a joy and privilege to witness yachts and schooners of great provenance once again crossing Nantucket Sound and entering Nantucket Harbor.

1, pg. 7; 2, pg. 38, A Brief History of Nantucket, the "little grey lady of the sea", Paul C. Morris, Maritime Nantucket, Lower Cape Publishing, Orleans, MA, 1996.

Neith, 1992.

A History of The Opera House Cup Race

Most people who have never heard of The Opera House Cup Race wonder what on earth an Opera House has to do with classic wooden yacht racing. The juxtaposition of the two metaphors can be disconcerting if one does not know the history of The Opera House Cup Race.

In 1946, when Harold Gaillard returned from World War II, he and his wife, Gwen, decided to open a restaurant on Nantucket. The name they chose, The Opera House, was meant to convey the idea that a restaurant could be more than just an eating establishment. It could become a center for community and cultural life, and that is exactly what happened.

Between 1946 and 1986 The Opera House was the most famous restaurant on Nantucket, decorated with some of Gwen Gaillard's personal antique collection and her opera posters, which covered the ceiling. The restaurant was known for its fine cuisine but also as a place to eat after a night on the town. It had the sophistication of a New York establishment but it catered to everyone. Some of the world's most famous celebrities, Judy Garland, Frank Sinatra, and Liz Taylor ate and entertained there. Great piano music could be heard spilling out onto the street played by the likes of Ralph Strain and Carl Norman. Many of the locals, especially sailors and boat builders, would wander into The Opera House to see old friends and catch up.

Over a period of 48 years, the Gaillards fulfilled their dream by putting together uniquely festive, intelligent and fun nightly social happenings. Including all of their friends, The Opera House family also extended to the community and far beyond the confines of the small island. When Harold died in 1972, Gwen was bereft; but by continuing to produce the magical ambiance in her restaurant, she kept herself alive and the spirit of what she and Harold had accomplished together.

One night during the summer of 1973, Gwen was approached by a group of serious sailors. They were owners of classic wooden yachts of some reknown. They were complaining that there were no races for vintage sailboats and wanted the opportunity to compete against each other. Gwen rose to the occasion, and said she would donate a winner's trophy and a dinner after the race. Thus was born the first classic yacht race on the East Coast of the United States.

Chick Walsh, who was managing The Opera House for Gwen, helped organize a race committee. It included Dick Deutsch, Hugh Sanford, and Joe Homer. Eric Urbahn created the handicapping system for the race, which is now used by the Wooden Boat Regatta Series. The course is set outside of Nantucket Harbor and can range from 16 to 28 miles depending on the wind and other weather conditions. No spinnakers are allowed on the down-wind leg.

That first year there were 13 entries, seven from Nantucket, and the rest from Martha's Vineyard, Newport, Rhode Island, and Connecticut. The winner of the first Opera House Cup Race was the young Bob Tiedeman who sailed up from Greenwich, Connecticut, in his father's 54-foot yawl, *Mariner*. During the past 26 years the race has grown substantially. By the late 1970s there were as many as 60 entrants and by the 1980s there were 75 entrants. Gwen's After-Race dinner, originally held at The Opera House, was moved to the shipyard because of the hundreds of people involved in the race. When The Opera House closed in 1986, Gwen personally sponsored the race the following summer to keep it going. For the past decade corporate sponsors, donations from individuals, and entry fees from participants have supported the race. Now there is a large gallery of spectators, some on the shore, standing by the lighthouse at the Brandt Point entrance to Nantucket Harbor, but mostly afloat in every kind of excursion boat. Impressive yachts like *Mandalay*, owned by Nelson Doubleday, Tommy Taylor's *Gleam* (named after the 12 Meter), and the classic motor yacht, *Pearl Necklace* from Newport add to the pageantry of the day. Airplanes swoop overhead capturing aerial photographs of the race, while press boats photograph the race, trying not to interfere.

The race now represents many different racing classes important in American yachting history. In 1979 the rule that sailboats had to be at least 32 feet in length was altered so that the Nantucket built Alerions, 26-feet overall, could be included. These delightful smaller crafts are reproductions of a Nathanael Herreshoff design; the first built was named *Alerion*. Sailboats range in size from the Alerions to the 120-foot J Boat *Shamrock V*. There are Concordias, Aldens, Sparkman and Stevens designs, schooners, and many Herreshoff designs of different vintages, such as the New York 30s and 40s, and the Alerions. *When and If*, the famous Alden schooner designed for General George Patton, is a regular contender. The U.S. 12 Meters have their own racing start. There are usually at least five present for the race running the gamut from *Gleam* and *Northern Light* built in the 1930s, to *Heritage* and

Concordia yawl, *Harbinger*, 1990 winner of The Opera House Cup, finds a weekend home on Straight Wharf, a Solitary wooden hull against a backdrop of fiberglass, 1991.

Chick Walsh and Lawrence Warner enjoy a few yarns at the captains' meeting – an opportunity to greet old friends and get updates on the race course, 1989.

Valiant built in the 1970s. Even with the distinct difference in the ages of these yachts, *Gleam* (with owner Bob Tiedeman at the helm) has been able to capture the cup three times in '79, '85 and '87, *Valiant* won twice in '91 and '92, *American Eagle* in '88 and *Heritage* in '93 and 2000. In 1998 there were 10 US 12s competing!

The rules of The Opera House Cup Race, much like those of the establishment for which it was named, tend to be inclusive. Criterion for entry does not discriminate about the age of the boat only specifying that it be a wooden monohull design. With the handicap system each sailboat has a chance to win. In fact, each year's winner is given an additional handicap penalty to limit its possibility of winning two years in succession. This spreads out the field allowing other boats a chance to win the Cup. In 1994, one of the most exciting wins, however, was the Nathanael Herreshoff's design, *Bambino*; a 42-foot sloop built in 1904!

Although most of the boats are restored (many were built pre-World War II and are now considered antique yachts), there are a few new boats being built. A new Alerion is under construction at this writing. There has been some consternation over the inclusion of "high-tech" designs with carbon fiber masts and spars, and cold-molded hulls, etc. In 1998 whatever issues existed were reconciled by creating a separate category for these new designs in the handicap race. Called "The Spirit of Tradition Class", it includes an interesting variety of yachts. Among them is *Grey Wolf*, a 40-foot sloop designed for The Opera House Cup Race in 1996 by Roger Martin and built by Lyman Morse in Thomaston, Maine in 1998. Another first of its kind is the W-Class racing yacht, *Wild Horses*, a 76-foot sloop inspired by the Herreshoff New York 50s and built for Donald Tofias. Joel White, owner of Brooklyn Boatyard in Rockport, Maine, was her designer.

Another change in 1998 is the inclusion of the Nantucket Island Community Sailing program in the management of The Opera House Cup Race. This adds a new dimension to the race, as the mission of the Community Sailing Program is to provide the island with affordable sailing instruction. The winner of the 1997 Opera House Cup Race, *Brilliant*, was used in 1998, as a training vessel for ten young sailors from Nantucket in order to compete in the race. Unfortunately 1998 made history because of lack of wind. For the first time the race was called and the expectant team of ten were unable to finish. Oh well, there's always next year!

Of the Classic Yacht Race series The Opera House Cup Race stands alone as the mother of all the races. Those who run The Opera House Cup Race today are perpetuating the spirit of The Opera House and its proprietors, Gwen and Harold Gaillard, by reaching out to the many sectors of the Nantucket community in an egalitarian manner. There is no question that the race is a beautiful singular example of an aesthetic slice of life that can be enjoyed by anyone interested. After 28 years, it still inspires interest and excitement. And now with a new generation of sailors actively involved in the race, the future still looks bright as ever for The Opera House Cup Race!

The Opera House Cup Race Starts and Courses

Starts

1st Start
12:00-*Warning*-white cylinder
12:05-*Preparatory*-blue cylinder
12:10-*Start*-red cylinder

2nd Start
12:15-*Warning*-white cylinder
12:20-*Preparatory*-blue cylinder
12:25-*Start*-red cylinder

3rd Start
12:30-*Warning*-white cylinder
12:35-*Preparatory*-blue cylinder
12:40-*Start*-red cylinder

Courses

1. "A"–Long Course SW/SE (29.9)
X to Z—3.8 n. miles @43° (P)*
Z to C—3.5 n. miles @ 350° (P)
C to A—3.8 n. miles @ 256° (P)
A to Z—5.0 n. miles @ 12° (P)
C to Z—3-5 n. miles @ 350° (P)
C to Z—3.5 n. miles @ 170° (S)
Z to X—6.8 n. miles @ 223°

2. "B"–Long Course NE/SE (19.9)
X to Z—3.8 n. miles @ 43° P)*
Z to C—3.5 n. miles @ 350° (P)
C to A—3.8 n. miles @ 256° (P)
A to Z—5.0 n. miles @ 120° (S)
Z to X—3.8 n. miles @ 223°*

3 . "C"–Long Course SW (20.2)
X to A—5.6 n. miles @ 342° (S)*
A to B—2.7 n. miles @ 347° S)
B to C—4.6 n. miles @ 111° (S)
C to Z—3.5 n. miles @ 170° (S)
Z to X—3.8 n. miles @ 223°*

4 . "D"–Long Course SW (22.9)
X to C—6.8 n. miles @ 020° (P)*
C to B—4.6 n. miles @ 291° (P)
B to A—2.7 n. miles @ 167° (P)
A to Z—5.0 n. miles @ 120° (S)
Z to X—3.8 n. miles @ 223°*

5. "E"–Medium Course NE (19.4)
X to C—6.8 n. miles @ 020° (P)*
C to A—3.8 n. miles @ 256° (P)
A to Z—5.0 n. miles @ 120° (S)
Z to X—3.8 n. miles @ 223°*

6. "F"–Medium Course SW (16.7)
X to A—5.6 n. miles @ 342° (S)
A to C—3.8 n. miles @ 76° (S)
C to Z—3.5 n. miles @ 170° (S)
Z to X—3.8 n. miles @ 223°*

7. "G"–Medium Course NE (16.7)
X to Z—3.8 n. miles @ 43° (P)*
Z to C—3.5 n. miles @ 350° (P)
C to A—3.8 n. miles @ 256° (P)
A to Z—5.6 n. miles @ 161°*

8. "S"–Short Course SW (14.4)
X to A—5.6 n. miles @ 342° (S)*
A to Z—5.0 n. miles @ 120° (S)
Z to X—3.8 n. miles @ 223°*

9. "S/B"–Short Course NE (14.4)
X to Z—3.8 n. miles @ 43° (P)*
Z to A—5.0 n. miles @ 300° (P)
A to X—5.6 n. miles @ 161°*

*All course headings to and from (X) are subject to change depending on actual location of start/finish line.
**All courses are magnetic. Distances accurate to 0.1 nautical mile. Courses to be signaled approximately 15 minutes prior to the first cylinder by a code flag (letter) on bow of committee boat.
***Marks to starboard (S), marks to port (P).

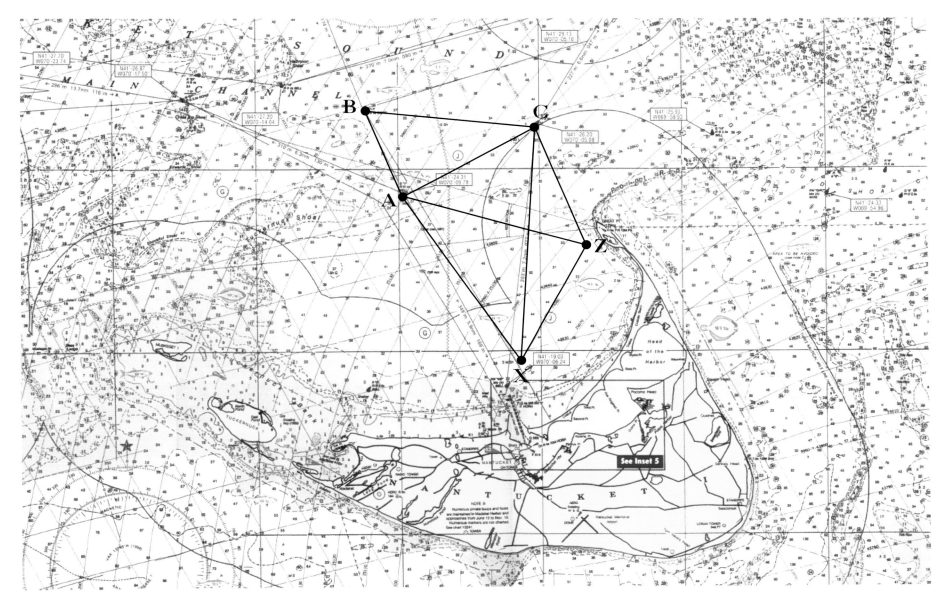

Nantucket with The Opera House Cup Race courses.

Lucy McDonald finds a seat on the boom, while her father, Courtland McDonald, prepares
Prospect of Whitby for a shakedown cruise the day before the race, 1996.

A schooner readies for the race, 1991.

When and If heads out to the race course, 1995.

Gwen leaves for the race on *Zorra*, 1992.

The *Uncatena*, a familiar sight to Nantucket visitors and residents, makes an unveering course for the mainland, 1989.

Spectators watch from the beach at Brandt's Point as the yachts leave for the race, 1995.

Picture postcards from years past show the Rainbow Fleet, a summer staple of visual pleasure, seen regularly off Nantucket shores, 1997.

The fleet approaches the starting line, 1983.

The bowmen on *Northern Light,* 1993 (above) and *American Eagle*, 1996 (right) during pre-start maneuvers
keep a vigilant eye out for yachts to starboard and leeward that might come perilously close.

A Hairy Moment at the Start of the "A" Class, Opera House Cup Race, 1994

"I first saw *Impala* in 1955. She would sail over to Nantucket a few times each summer and anchor in the harbor. Then, if there were five yachts in, it was a busy day and the harbor considered full! Even back in the fifties, when all the boats were pretty, *Impala* was considered a special beauty. Little did I know I would own her someday." These are the proud words of Alfie Sanford who took ownership of the yacht in 1986 after many years of loving her from afar.

Impala, built in 1953 is a 57-foot Sparkman and Stevens design yawl, built by Abeking and Rassmussen in Lemwerder, Germany. Her lines are a development of the *Stormy Weather* design and show the influence of John Alden in her hull design and interior layout. After a career of racing on the West Coast as well as the East Coast and a few years in the 70s spent in the Caribbean, Nantucket is now her home. Alfie Sanford has raced *Impala* in The Opera House Cup Race every year since he bought her in 1986. He has also taken her on cruises to the Caribbean, Bermuda, Nova Scotia, Prince Edwards Island, Newfoundland, Dominican Republic, Cuba, Chesapeake, Turks, Caicos, and the Bahamas. For an old girl, she really gets around!

The following sequence of photographs shows *Impala* at the start of the race in 1994. As *Impala* heads for the pin at the starting line, a 38-foot sloop, *Wind*, intercepts her. Impala has the right of way but ends up ensnared by a stay from the smaller craft, which keeps the two yachts bound together in a dangerous dance of scraping and jarring movements until they can disentangle themselves and continue. *Wind* was disqualified from the race but *Impala* went on to finish 16th out of 67 boats entered that year. Not bad considering the initial hangup. *Ticonderoga's* mast snapped the same year and the 12 Meter, *Intrepid* ran into the jetty located near the harbor entrance. It wasn't exactly a smooth day for sailing.

The start of Class A, in which staying inside the orange marker becomes an aggressive art, 1994.

The start of the 12 Meters, 1994.

J Boat, *Shamrock V* and the 12 Meter, *Gleam*...

...race past Great Point, 1994.

Shamrock V and crew taken to task, 1995.

"ESSENCE OF J…"

Elizabeth Meyer is dedicated to the restoration of wooden boats large and small. Her love of wooden boats started at an early age sailing with her parents and flourished as she grew up sailing yachts of all sizes. Restoration of wooden yachts became her passion as she consulted clients on their projects as well as her own. She founded the International Yacht Restoration School in Newport, Rhode Island, whose purpose is to teach the skills of restoration to future generations and to preserve a part of our maritime history afloat. She believes that working with one's hands as a shipwright is an honorable profession indispensable to yacht preservation.

She bought the J-boat, *Endeavour*, in 1984 and started the 4-year restoration in 1985. She bought and maintained *Shamrock V* in the 1990s. *Shamrock* was built in 1939 for Sir Thomas Lipton and exists today as the only wooden J-boat still afloat. In 1997 she was sold by Elizabeth and has since been going through a major restoration in England.

When asked to describe what makes J-boats stand apart from all the other racing yachts, she says "Essence of J…You feel as if you're on a 130-foot ironing board in the middle of the ocean!" She is, of course, describing the largest and grandest of all classic racing yachts. Her restoration of *Shamrock V* kept the esthetics of the yacht intact while incorporating new materials such as a carbon fiber mast, an aluminum boom, and hydraulic winches. Her feeling is that there is nothing wrong with using new materials as long as the look of the yacht is kept authentic.

Anyone who has ever witnessed a classic yacht regatta will attest to the fact that there is nothing more magnificent than the sight of a J-boat sailing at about 14 knots, mowing through the waves like a knife cutting through butter.

Shamrock V in fog, 1996.

THE 12 METERS

12 Meters start, 2000.

BOB TIEDEMANN

*B*ob Tiedemann and his wife, Elizabeth, are here pictured hard at work with their crew members preparing *Gleam* for the first leg of the race. Bob is a purist when it comes to boat preservation. He is particularly interested in saving classic yachts from "the chain saw," and believes in the integrity of restoration as, "We are preserving history…this is the Real McCoy."

To date Bob has preserved two pre-World War II 12 Meter yachts, *Northern Light* and *Gleam*. Both boats figure in Rosenfeld's famous photograph, "Flying Spinnakers", taken in 1939. He has also restored 62-foot commuter Rum Runner, *Pam*, built in 1921, and *Lalegro*, built in 1918. He found *Pam* "languishing" in Fort Lauderdale, before bringing her back to life. The Tiedemans also own and maintain Bob's father's yacht, *Mariner*, the 54-foot yawl that won the first Opera House Cup Race in 1973, and again in 1978. The yachts make up a charter fleet which Bob and Elizabeth run out of Newport, Rhode Island. The proceeds of their business enable them to keep up the costly job of maintenance and to pursue their passionate commitment to the preservation of classic yachts.

When asked what turns him on about the 12 Meters, Bob remarked, "You're right down there and the water is hissing past your shoulder. The sound of the water is as good a gauge of speed as anything."

Bob and Elizabeth Tiedeman with crew, 1995.

Gleam, 1993.

Northern Light, 2000.

Heritage, 1994.

Eastener, 2000.

THE 12 METERS OF GEORGE HILL AND HERB MARSHALL

Who in their right mind would take on the restoration and maintenance of a 30 to 50 year old wooden boat of at least 60 feet? One would imagine that such a person would have to be wealthy at least with an income vast enough to support the constant repairs and refurbishment of these aging beauties: face lifts, tummy tucks, major operations to keep all systems working. Take the financial requirements of an aging relative and multiply times 10 and one might be dollars and cents in the same ballpark. So why would someone take on such a responsibility? Yacht racing has always been considered a rich man's sport. With enough discretionary income on hand the sometimes staggering cost was of little consequence.

Today, however, the owners of many of the 12 Meter racers are not wealthy men. They are people who have decided to follow their bliss to create personal lifestyles, which allow them the freedom to be on the ocean doing what they love most–sailing some of the finest yachts ever built and preserving them as floating examples of maritime history, providing hands-on connections with our seafaring past. Among such owners are George Hill and Herb Marshall. Independent of one another, they started pursuing their passion about 11 years ago. George purchased *Weatherly*, the America's Cup contender, and Herb bought *American Eagle*, built in 1964, previously owned and raced by Ted Turner.

George Hill and his wife found *Weatherly* in Seattle, Washington, in 1986. He describes the yacht as being in sad condition. In September of that year they purchased the boat relying on the basically sound structure of the hull and spent the next six weeks preparing her to go offshore. The engine wasn't working and there was black sludge in the bilge. On and on went the list of minor repairs. Much had to be accomplished to clean up the great lady for the trip through the Panama Canal to Florida and eventually back to Newport.

The trip to Panama commenced in early November, but they lost the rudder in the Pacific. They ended up going 250 miles with a sheet of plywood jury-rigged as a rudder. The boat needed to be hauled in Acapulco for repairs. George and his wife had run out of money before they reached the Canal. Some friends came to the rescue, enabling them to continue their journey. They arrived in Florida in mid-February and in early March of 1987 the boat was hauled out for some cosmetic repairs in preparation for the scheduled sail north in May. While the boat was being picked up on the lift, the cross beam on the traveler broke and the bow of *Weatherly* crashed down on the cement, severing the leg of the lift driver. It was a tragic accident and the shipyard offered to take full responsibility for damages to the worker and the yacht. *Weatherly* was put in dry dock where some work was done on her until August of 1987.

Yet the boatyard where the accident occurred was not forthcoming with the appropriate funds, and George was again running out of money. He took a loan on his car to generate the cash necessary to once again jury-rig the boat and patch the bow in order for *Weatherly* to be brought to Newport before the oncoming winter. Again funds were needed. George's father came forth and put his home up as collateral for a loan to cover the rebuilding and restoration of *Weatherly*. By June of 1988, almost two years from the time of her rescue, *Weatherly* was able to sail.

She is now used as a charter boat in Newport, as is *American Eagle*. Herb and George now are in business together. *Nefertiti*, built in 1982 by Ted Hood, was their first joint effort. They brought her back to the US from South Africa in 1996. In the spring of 1998 they launched a fully restored *Intrepid* to join their ranks. Built in 1968, *Intrepid* won the America's Cup twice and was the last wooden hull 12 Meter ever built. When asked what drives Herb to restore these boats he replied, "It's about stopping. It feels so good when you stop." When pushed on the point, neither Herb nor George seems to know why they do what they do, but it is obvious that they enjoy every minute of their continuing adventure with 12 Meters. Herb and George together run America's Cup Charters out of Newport that also represents *Columbia*, America's Cup winner 1958, and *Heritage*, Charlie Morgan's 1970 contender, as well as the J boats, *Endeavor* and *Shamrock V*. George says that chartering allows many people the opportunity of sailing these yachts whom otherwise could not individually afford to do so. Chartering is a way for these yachts to pay their own way and afford their owners a life of sailing and pursuing their passion.

Valiant and *Weatherly*, 1993.

Valiant and *Weatherly*, 1993.

Nefertiti, 2000.

American Eagle, 1991.

Harbinger

Harbinger is one of the Concordia Yawls built between 1938 and 1965. All 103 yachts are still intact today, which testifies to the popularity of the design. Lawrence and Susie Warner have owned *Harbinger* since 1978. Lawrence knows every bolt and screw that keeps *Harbinger* fastened and he maintains her impeccably.

Harbinger won The Opera House Cup Race in 1990 and would have won the following year if it hadn't been for the handicap system. When a boat wins, its handicap is changed to make it more difficult for the same boat to succeed again. Lawrence feels that this is a fair rule and although he would love to have gone home with the silver twice in a row, says he believes the handicap process gives a chance to a wider variety of participants.

Lawrence and Susie Warner and their crew aboard their Concordia yawl *Harbinger* try to outstrip *Valiant* on the windward leg. Hurricane Bob blew in with a vengeance the next day, 1991.

Fortune,1994.

FORTUNE

*F*or $800 plus an "S" boat and a Beetle Cat, Don Glassie bought a much-abused *Fortune* in 1975. Don first spied the barely floating *Fortune* in Newport Harbor with a "For Sale" sign on her. It wasn't until she was sitting in dry dock in Marion, Massachusetts, that he could see her underbelly. It was then he decided to bite the bullet, and trade his beloved "S" boat for the boat he had had nightmares about. In a dream he thought "Oh my God, I can't deal with that boat. It will twist in half."

That boat, *Fortune*, was originally built in 1926 in a yard in Somerset, Massachusetts. She was designed by B.B. Crownenshield and was one of the first modern staysail rigged schooners. With 50 feet on deck and a beam of 9'8", she narrows radically as the sides approach the keel. Her underbody was advanced for her time and her keel has iron on the bottom. She was originally well built but comparatively light. The hull is versatile: it could be rigged as a yawl as an alternative to the schooner rig.

Fortune has been around. Under previous ownership she spent time in the Great Lakes. She was raced to Bermuda at least eight times, but her final trip was aborted when a wave hit and broke the bumpkin. At one time she was impounded in Cuba under the Castro regime.

Now under Don Glassie's watchful eye, she has been restored to her original specifications using B.B. Crownenshield's plans, which now belong to the Peabody Museum in Salem, Massachusetts. Don claims that once you learn how to maintain a wooden boat, it may be the cheapest way to have a great boat. If maintained properly, a wooden boat will always hold up well. He feels there needs to be more interest in wooden yacht restoration in the United States, that the European restorers are soaking up a lot of American boats. "It would be nice if our boats stayed here."

What Don likes about The Opera House Cup Race is the "go for it" attitude of the competitors. He thinks the race has the best party in the Classic Yacht Regatta Series. He calls it "A Big Good Time." In his book Gwen Gaillard is "Absolutely Great!" He tells a story of going to a Nantucket thrift shop and buying a bull fighter poster and a pink boudoir chair. While trying to stuff the items down the front hatch of *Fortune*, Gwen walked by and said, "Don, I see you're a collector. I've got some stuff you might like. Why don't you come by for a drink?" That was the beginning of their friendship.

What does Don want? To win The Opera House Cup again!

Fortune, 1992.

PROSPECT OF WHITBY

This 42-foot mahogany sloop was commissioned by an Englishman, Arthur Slater in 1964 as an Admiral's Cup Contender in England, and in that year won the Admiral's Cup. *Prospect of Whitby* was the first of five *Prospects* built for Slater. Designed by Sparkman and Stephens and built by Bjarn As in Norway, *Prospect* boasts single-planked, edge-glued construction over oak frames. The design and construction was extremely high-tech for the time. Lawrence Smart, an English shipwright by trade, found her languishing in a storage barn in Belgium where she had been for 10 years. Familiar with her history, he bought and restored *Prospect* in 1984. He brought her to where she now resides on Buzzard's Bay in Marion with her new owners, Courtland and Georgia McDonald.

Prospect of Whitby, 1996.

Ticonderoga, 2000.

HERRESHOFF

*F*ounded By John Brown Herreshoff in 1863, the Herreshoff Manufacturing Company of Bristol, Rhode Island, is best known for its custom yachts and one design classes. Nathanael Herreshoff, younger brother of J.B., built five of the eight America's Cup defenders which captured the prize between 1893 and 1934. This established the Herreshoffs as premier American yacht designers and builders. The name Herreshoff became synonymous with brilliance in yachting architecture and construction worldwide.

Nathanael Herreshoff, trained as an engineer at M.I.T., was a legend in his time for creating speed in sailing vessels. His boats were the racing machines of their day. He incorporated the most innovative materials to hasten his creations to victory at the finish line. His son, L. Francis Herreshoff, continued the tradition and added an aesthetic quality so distinctive that today he is considered to have created wooden yacht design as art form. *Ticonderoga* is an example of his poetry in motion.

Today among the graceful small craft seen off the shores of Cape Cod and the Islands are the Herreshoff 12$\frac{1}{2}$ footers, the Alerions, and the S boats. All three are raced in fleets at various yacht clubs in the southern New England area.

THE ALERIONS

The smallest class in The Opera House Cup Race, the 26-foot Alerion is a reproduction of a Nathanael Herreshoff design of a pleasure craft he built for himself. He experimented with the yacht off the coast of Bermuda whence it was shipped by steamship to sail in the lagoons around the island. Because they are such extreme shoal draft sailing yachts, Alerions have been adopted as a Nantucket racing class.

Vintage, Orthia and *Owl*, 1991.

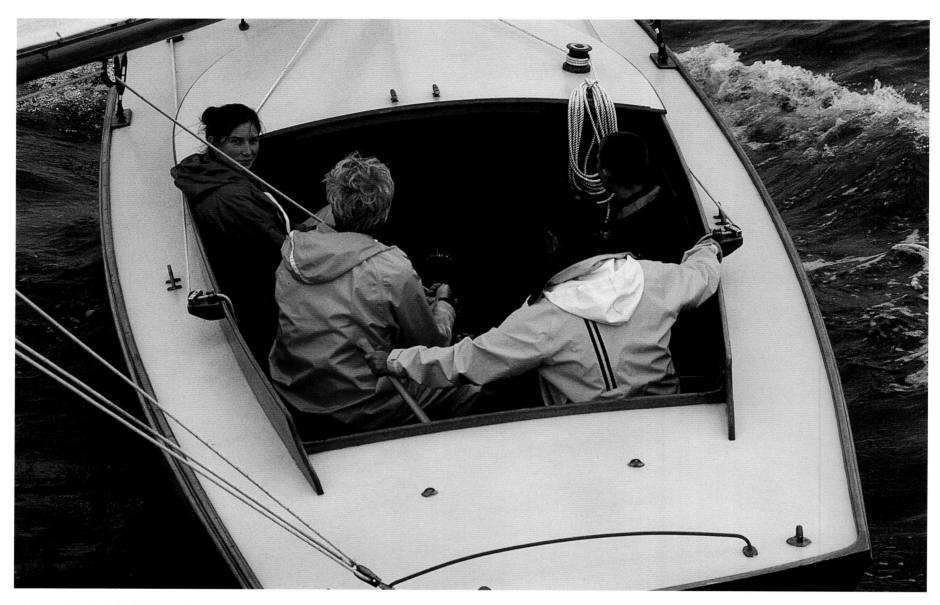

Alerions – Nantucket delights, 1992.

Feathers on the water, 1993.

Built in 1904, *Bambino*, a Herreshoff design forunner of the New York 30 design, heads out for the race. Winner of The Opera House Cup Race in 1994, she was the oldest participant in that race. This sloop has proven that smaller yachts, less geared for racing, can beat the 12 Meters using the handicap system.

Bambino, 2000 (left) and 1993 (above).

RUGOSA

Rugosa, built in 1926 is a N.Y. 40. Nathanael Herreshoff designed her as part of a fleet for the New York Yacht Club. *Rugosa* won the Bermuda Race in 1928 and was rediscovered in Florida in the 1980s by members of the Herreshoff family. She was then bought and restored by Halsey Herreshoff, grandson of Nathanael. Many of the other Herreshoff designs are owned and raced by the Herreshoff Museum in Bristol. In 2001 *Rugosa* celebrated her 75th year by being refitted stem to stern. In the Summer of 2001 she crossed the Atlantic with Halsey at the helm to participate in the America's Cup Jubilee celebration of the 150th Anniversary of the America's Cup.

Rugosa, 1996.

Changing jibs...

Neith, 1996.

When and If, 1996.

WHEN AND IF

*I*n Vineyard Haven, Martha's Vineyard, there is a boatyard called Gannon and Benjamin. It has been in existence for the past 21 years. What started on a hope and some promise, has become a year-round profitable venture of Ross Gannon and his partner, Nat Benjamin.

They wanted desperately to provide a yard where wooden boat owners could work on their own yachts with the assistance of boatyard expertise and back up. They thought that this was a worthwhile cause and their first choice in how they wanted to spend their time, but they did not think it could be a livelihood. They tried desperately for several years to acquire $5000 start-up money from friends and associates to begin their dream, but no one came forth with the monies to fund them. One day a relative who had sold some property in Crested Butte, Colorado said he had $5000 that he was willing to risk on their venture. Ross and Nat assumed that they would have a seasonal business and that they would have to support their families with other endeavors like fishing. But to their surprise the business flourished and they have more than enough work to keep them busy year-round.

Among their adventures has been the restoration of *When and If*. Commissioned by General George Patton, the schooner was launched in 1939. He used the yacht very little because he was sent overseas in 1941, hence the name, *When and If*, as he wasn't sure what the outcome would be. After the war in 1945 he was killed in a car accident, but his family kept the boat until 1971, donating it to the Landmark School in Manchester, Massachusetts. The Patton family chose the Landmark School because it is a school for children with learning disabilities. It had been presumed that George Patton would have been diagnosed with such a disability if the knowledge of said learning disorders had existed in his time.

A terrible storm hit the Northeast Coast in October of 1991. *When and If* had been under contract for sale at that time, but as a result of five days of battering winds and seas, the vessel ended up on the rocks in Pride's Crossing, Massachusetts. By chance Ross Gannon was in the neighborhood a few days after the storm and he reports seeing *When and If* lying on the rocks with a hole on her port side so large "a car could fit into it." The new owner was at a loss as to whether he could afford the restoration of the wreckage, which had once been a gallant schooner. Soon a remarkable collaboration was negotiated sealing the future of the vessel. The new owner committed himself to the purchase of the wreck and in partnership with the boatyard, Gannon and Benjamin was able to afford the restoration and maintenance of the yacht. They moved her by barge from Manchester to Martha's

Vineyard and for three winters Ross and Nat labored to restore the yacht to her original state. After three long years, *When and If* was ready to be relaunched and has raced in The Opera House Cup ever since.

Like many other restored wooden yachts, *When and If* now earns her keep by being chartered. How wonderful for everyone to be able to share in this little piece of history. When asked about how one goes about such an undertaking as this restoration, Ross Gannon replied, "One piece at a time." Patterns have to be made for each fitting and they are replicated as close as possible to the original hardware.

This was not Gannon and Benjamin's first major restoration. They had bought the 72-foot yacht, *Zorra*, at an insurance auction in Norfolk, Virginia. Designed by Renato Levi and built in Italy in 1967, *Zorra* was declared a total loss when the afterdeck had been burned off in a fire and the cockpit was burned out. It took Ross and Nat eight years to restore the yacht "piece by piece," and she is now a magnificent tribute to their craft and skill. Jim Feeney bought *Zorra* in 1996 and renamed her *Kathleen* after his wife. Aside from changing the color from black to white, some exterior upkeep and interior redecorating, the yacht is unchanged from the original design. She is now moored in Sippican Harbor in Marion, and chartered on various occasions.

Gannon and Benjamin do not believe in changing the original designs of the boats that they restore to make them faster racing vessels. Ross says that winning classic yacht regattas is low on his list of priorities. Yet Nat Benjamin has constructed new wooden updated versions of some older designs like *Tern*, designed after L. Francis Herreshoff's Rozzinante design.

Zorra, 1995.

Kathleen, 2000.

Kathleen, 1996.

Tern, 1996, is an updated reproduction designed by Nat Benjamin of Benjamin and Gannon, Martha's Vineyard.

In 1931 Eastern Shipbuilding Corporation of Shelbourne, Nova Scotia built *Christmas,* a 45-foot W. Starling Burgess design. Phillip LaFrance captained her in the Caribbean in the 1970s, then bought her and from 1979 to 1984 restored her in Marion. She was bought and redesigned in 1993 by Donald Tofias under the name of *Arawak*. At this writing she is for sale with her named changed back to *Christmas.*

Christmas, 2000 (left) and as *Arawak*, 1994 (above).

CHANGE OF WEATHER
REPLICAS

*E*very now and then a yacht is created that is so distinctive in design that it is sought after by many. There have been a myriad of "reproductions" over the years of one-design class boats like the Alerions and the Rozinantes etc., but the larger one-of-a-kind vessels are not only excessively expensive to recreate but take the passion, patience and expertise delegated only to a select few.

Two examples of reproductions of the famous yacht, *Ticonderoga*, are *Whitehawk*, a 92-foot version built in the 1970s, and *Radiance*, built in the 1990s to the exact length of *"Ti."* Both are modern in materials but stay faithful to the original L. Francis Herreshoff design.

Ticonderoga and her replica *Radiance* choose separate tacks at the first mark, 1996.

Whitehawk and *Glide*, 2000.

The old and the new – *Whitehawk* and *Bambino*, 2000.

In Search of the Next Mark

When and If follows the fleet, 1996.

NEW WOODEN YACHT DESIGNS

*D*esigned by Roger Martin and built by Lyman Morse of Thomaston, Maine, in 1996, *Gray Wolf* is a 40-foot sloop of stripped planked cedar, covered with a layer of fiberglass cloth and epoxy resin. It has an unstayed carbon fiber mast with only running backstays to adjust the luff and tension of the jib. A steel fin keel with a lead weighted bulb gives the hull stability. The light and strong design is advertised as a "state-of-the-art", and "soon-to-be-a-classic" design. Eric Urbahn originally owned her and she now resides with a private owner. The Opera House Cup Race encourages yacht designers and builders to create new wooden vessels to perpetuate the classic tradition.

Gray Wolf leading the pack, 1996.

THE W-CLASS YACHTS

Donald Tofias developed a new racing class of 76-foot sloops, designed by Joel White. The W-Class has the look of everything classic but is new in construction and technology. Based on the Herreshoff NY 50 design, the "W"s are long, sleek and elegant. Joel White's son, Steve White, built the first of its kind launched in 1998, *Wild Horses*, at Brooklyn Boatyard in Brooklyn, Maine. The same year John England built *White Wings* the sister yacht at Rockport Marine, Rockport, Maine. In 2000 two smaller 46-foot versions, *Equus* and *Zebra*, were also built there.

The W-Class yachts are esthetically pleasing inside and out. The interiors are fitted out in cherry wood giving them a rich, warm feeling. Great attention is paid to detail such as the tiny "W"s carved into the woodwork, and the gilt "W" logo chiseled by hand and gilded into the boatstripe. The hulls are constructed of cold-molded wood, which enhances their lightness and strength. Donald believes in relying on reusable resources whenever possible. W-Class sloops veer from classic design in that the underbodies are designed with spade rudders and fin keels. He has no doubt that if Nathanael Herreshoff was alive today, his designs would take into consideration all of the most innovative technology.

The W-Class is built to race as a one-design yacht. *Wild Horses* and *White Wings* are the only two in existence at this writing. Because they are new yachts with technological updates to traditional design, they race in the Spirit of Tradition class. Donald believes in resurgence of "big" wooden yacht racing and has committed himself financially and creatively into making his passion a reality.

Donald with crew on stern of *Wild Horses,* 1998.

White Wings, 2000.

White Wings and *Wild Horses*, 2000.

Becalmed

1992

12 Meters at slow start, 1998 (above and right).

Alabama, 1998.

Whitehawk, 1998.

Heritage and *Valiant* wait for a wind or tide change, 1992.

Inch by inch, foot by foot. *Valiant*, 1992.

The finish gun. *Valiant*, 1992.

Time to celebrate. *Valiant,* 1992.

A faster finish. *Vortex* and *Harbinger*, 1994.

Prospect of Whitby sailing home, 1994.

WAITING FOR RESULTS

The Opera House Cup Party, 1989.

A banquet from the sea quenches lusty appetites
and leaves fingers sticky with salt, 1989.

Nothing like a brew or a chilled chardonnay to whet the old whistle! 1989.

Gwen with award, 1989.

Devotion and gratitude – Gwen Galliard awards the cup
to Don Glassie, skipper of *Fortune*, 1989.

Crew accepting award, 1992.

Valiant crew in crowd, 1992.

A new location: In 1999 the party was moved to Jettie's Beach to accommodate the increase in the crowd, 2000.

And the beat goes on...hopefully for future generations, 2000.

To be continued... 2000 to?

AFTERWORD

This is our story of The Opera House Cup Race. We have enjoyed every minute of chronicalling and researching, but mostly of just experiencing this race annually. We are aware that our perspective is ours and that it does not reflect many anecdotes and memories, which are precious to many others who have been more involved with the race and have participated for as long as or longer than we have. There are many more stories about The Opera House Cup Race that could not possibly fit into one book. We would like to take this opportunity to thank all the participants and apologize to those whose names and yachts have been left out of this edition. We are aware that we have not given these competitors worthy acknowledgement, which is one of the shortcomings of being two people trying to complete a book in four years. We hope that with the success of this small effort we will be able to provide more information about other yachts and their owners in future editions.

Sincerely,

Annie Converse and Camie Ford

Endeavour, 2000.

Opera House Cup winners in boatshed, 1992.

Past Opera House Cup Winners

1973 MARINER	1982 BANZAI	1991 VALIANT
1974 PIERA	1983 WHITEHAWK	1992 VALIANT
1975 CHOICE	1984 LEGEND	1993 HERITAGE
1976 ESCAPADE	1985 GLEAM	1994 BAMBINO
1977 ELSKE	1986 BRILLIANT	1995 HIGH COTTON
1978 MARINER	1987 GLEAM	1996 PIERA
1979 GLEAM	1988 AMERICAN EAGLE	1997 BRILLIANT
1980 ESCAPADE	1989 FORTUNE	1998 NO RACE
1981 FORTUNE	1990 HARBINGER	1999 NAIAD

2000
HERITAGE

2001
WEATHERLY

GLOSSARY

Aft: The back end of a boat, opposite the bow also called its stern.

Afterdeck: A weather deck toward the stern of a yacht's midship.

Alerion: A 26-foot sailboat designed by Nathanael Herreshoff for himself as a pleasure boat. It is reproduced in wood in Nantucket and fiberglass in Rhode Island.

Barge: Freighter or freight excursion boat, generally double-decked, with no motor and intended to be towed.

Bilge: The portion of the boat extending outward from her keel, the lowest portion of a boat inside the hull.

Boom: A spar used to spread a fore and aft sail from the gooseneck to the foot of the sail.

Bumpkin: A small outrigger or spar extending over a boat's stern, as in a yawl, to which a mizzen sheet attaches.

Carbonfiber: A metal material used to make masts and booms in modern day yachts. Preferred by some builders and designers for its lightness and durability.

Cockpit: A sunken space in the deck usually toward the stern or midsection of a boat accommodating skipper and crew and allowing access to the cabin.

Coldmolded: A modern process sometimes used in the construction of wooden boats, which creates multiple layers of wood to make one solid piece for the hull.

Crew: A company of men and women, below the officers rank, who perform assigned tasks for a boat.

Current: A progressive motion of the water caused by a rising or receding tide, or by movement of prevailing wind upon the sea.

Drydock: Used in describing a boat on land to be repaired or stored.

Epoxy Resin: A strong bonding substance used in boat construction.

Finkeel: A type of keel used in racing yachts to increase lateral resistance in sailing and supply ballasting in the lowest possible position.

Fitting: A piece of machinery or article permanently installed on a boat.

Fleet: A group of boats under a single command, similarly involved such as in a race.

Handicap: "Yacht racing in which boats are allowed an advantage specified in time or distance, depending upon departure from a standard sail area, size or type of rig." Pg. 219

Hank: "A U-shaped fitting used to secure a luff of a jib or staysail to its stay or luff of a gaff sail hoisted on a traveller." Pg. 219

Hardware: A term used to describe particular pieces of machinery or metal fittings on a boat.

Hull: Body of a boat below the deck housings and riggings.

J Boat: A class of racing yachts, approximately 120 feet designed in the 1930s to race for the America's Cup.

Jib: Triangular-shaped sail set on a stay leading from jib-boom or bowsprit to the top foremasthead with its jib sheet extending to the winches in the cockpit.

Juryrig: A temporary makeshift of sails, masts, rigs, etc., to enable the boat to continue after damage or loss of equipment.

Keel: Main structure or support of a boat running longitudinally along the centerline of the bottom.

Ketch: A two masted sailboat with its forward mast taller than the aft mast or mizzen, which is located in front of the stern-post.

Launch: To set afloat a boat from land into a floating depth of water.

Leadweighted Bulb: Located on the end of a finkeel in certain newer designed sailboats to improve stability and handling of the boat.

Leeward: Direction away from which the wind is blowing.

Leg (of race): The distance sailed from one point to another.

Lift: A breeze that creates a sailboat to point higher into the wind.

L.O.A.: Length overall from the forward to the aft end of a boat.

Luff: To sail closer to or head the sailboat toward the wind, in order to slow her down, the sails are not full of air.

Mark: In racing, a buoy used to show the various legs of the racecourse.

Mast: A poll or spar of wood or metal supporting the sailboat's boom, and all the gear for spreading the sail.

12 Meter: A class of yachts designed to compete for the America's Cup.

Monohull: A sailboat design consisting of one hull.

New York 30 and 40: A class of wooden yachts designed by Nathanael Herreshoff.

Port: Looking forward on a boat, a term used to describe the left side.

Rozinante: A classic yacht designed by L. Francis Herreshoff.

Rudder: A vertical flat piece or structure of wood or metal used to steer a boat; fitted at the aft end of a boat immersed body.

Rumrunner: A classic wooden motor yacht.

Running Backstay: Located on both sides of the aft end of a sailboat used to secure the mast. When tacking, it is slacked on the leeward side and tightened on the windward side.

Schooner: A two-masted sailboat characterized by the fore-and-aft rig of her masts; the forward one being smaller in size than the one toward the stern.

Shakedown: A term used to familiarize captain and crew of the procedure and workings aboard a boat.

Shoal: A sandbank or bar from sea level when the depth is six fathoms or less.

Sloop: One masted fore-and-aft rigged sailboat, carrying a mainsail and one or more jibs, or in heavier craft a gaff-topsail.

Starboard: Looking forward on a boat, a term to describe the right side.

Staysail: A fore-and-aft sail, either in triangular or quadrilateral pattern, that is set "flying" and in no way connected with a stay.

Stern-post: "The heavy upright timber or bar at after extremity of the keel." Pg. 537

Tack: In sailing, direction of ship's heading with relation from where the wind is blowing, being on starboard or port tack. A term used when changing sailing direction going into the wind.

Tide: Alternate rise and fall of the ocean's surface due to the attraction of the sun and the moon.

Tiller: A strong piece of wood approximately three feet in length attached to the rudder shaft and used to steer the boat in place of a wheel.

Unstayed: Without stays supporting the mast.

Windward: In the direction from which the wind is blowing; toward the wind.

Yacht: Any craft other than fishing or trading boat used privately for official trips, or for racing.

Yawl: A two-masted fore-and-aft sailboat; the forward mast being taller than the aft mast called a mizzen, jigger or dandy and is located behind the stern-post.

BIBLIOGRAPHY

Encyclopedia of Nautical Knowledge, A.E. Lewis, and W.A. McEwen, Cornell Maritime Press, Centerville, MD, first edition, 1953, fourth edition, 1994.

A Brief History of the Herreshoff Marine Museum, The Impetus-The Herreshoff Manufacturing Company, Herreshoff Museum Publications, courtesy of Carol Bausch 2001.

A Pictorial History of Nantucket, the "little grey lady of the sea", Paul C. Morris, Maritime Nantucket, Lower Cape Publishing, Orleans, MA, 1996.

The Opera House Cup Race Program, 1996, 1997, 1998, 1999, 2000. "The Legend of the Race," Gene Mahon; "The First Opera Cup Race," "The Wood Will Meet the Wind," Barbara Lloyd; Terry Pommet

Page 3, reproduction of The Opera House Cup Race trophy and page 20, Starts and Courses, compliments of The Opera House Cup Race Committee.

INDEX OF PHOTOS OF BOATS

Past Opera House Cup Participants

Addie
Adrianne
Agnes
Aile Blanche
Alabama
Alemax
Alainora
Allise
Altair
American Eagle
Amorita
Angelita
Anoa
Antares
Arapaho
Arawak (yawl)
Arawak (cutter)
Archangel
Arethusa
Argonaut
Ariel
Aries
Arrowhead
Astraeus
Avenger
Ayesha
Ayuthia

Baccarat
Balara
Bambino
Banalore
Banicate
Banzai
Bapple
Beau Jangles
Beowulf
Blitzen
Blue Fox
Blue Goose
Boomerang
Brigadoon
Brilliant
Camelot
Carina
Caroler
Catrionam
Cetus
China Bird
Chips
Christmas
Christiania
Christina
Columbia
Comet

Consolation
Cool Running
Deifiant
Destiny
Diva
Easterner
Edith
Elsa
Elska
Endeavor
Equity
Estrella
Evening Solace
Falcon
Felicity
Fiddler's Green
Firebird
Firebrand
Fishhawk
Fleetwing
Flirt
Fomalhaut
Fortune
Friendship
Galatea
Gitana IV
Gjoa

Gleam
Glide
Goblin
Gone With The Wind
Goose
Gray Wolf
Green Dolphin
Half Moon
Harbinger
Harmony
Harvest
Heart's Desire
Henry
Heritage
Hesperus
High Cotton
Hindu
Hither 'Nyon
Hob Nob
Horizon
Hot Foot
Huntress
Hussar
Impala
Independent Man
Infanta
Interlude

Intrepid
Irene
Isabelle
Island Girl
Jane Dore III
Java
Juno
Kaikoura
Kanga
Karin
Kathleen
Ker Anna
Kestral
Lana & Harley
Lands End
Lap Wing
Lark
Latonka
Legend
Lely
Lethe
Liberty
L' iliade &L'odysse
Lindy
Loose Cannon
Louise
Madeline

Madrigal	New Way	Quest	Signe	Tomahawk
Madrigal II	Niam	Quiet Thunder	Sintra	Tusitala
Magic (26-foot alerion)	Nina	Radiance	Siren	Undina
Magic (29.5 sloop)	Northern Light	Realt Na Mara	Sisyphus	Valiant
Magic Carpet	Nyala	Red Baron	Slip Away	Varua
Malabar	Nyatonga	Reliance	Snipe	Vela
Manukai	O Scolomio	Restless	Snow Goose	Venture
Many Moons	Renda	Riptide	Snowgoose	Violet
Marauder	Oriane	Robin	Sonnet	Viva
Marie J	Orthia	Rosalind	Sou'wester	Vortex
Marin	Osprey	Rugosa	Stiletto	Weatherly
Mariner	Owl	S y Quest	Storm	Westray
Matinicus	Papajecco	Sally	Sumurun	When and If
Matoaka	Phalarope (sloop)	Salty	Susanna	Whisper
Mercury	Phalarope (ketch)	Sanity	Swallow	Whisper II
Mermaid	Phra Luang	Sapphire	Symfoni	White Wings (ketch)
Mischief	Physalia	Saudade	Synergy	White Wings (sloop)
Moon Shadow	Piear	Savage	Talisman	White Wings (76-foot sloop)
Moondrift	Pilot	Seabound	Tam 'O Shanter	Whitehawk
Moonspiner	Pollux	Sea Chanty	Tamarisk	Wind
Mya	Pride of Baltimore	Seguin	Tango II	Windblown
Naiad	Primadonna	Senta	Taygeta	Winflower
Natasha	Princess	Sequin	Tern	Windigo
Nayada	Prologue	Serendipity	T ethys	Wing On
Neaptide	Prospect of Whitby	Shamrock V	Ticonderoga	Ynys Bach
Nefertiti	Queequeg	Shimaera	Titia	Ziggurat
Neith	Querida of Howth	Shiris	Tivoli	Zorra